This book is dedicated to
my joy and yours :)

SWEET RHYMES FOR TRYING TIMES

SOCIAL EMOTIONAL LEARNING | FEELINGS AND EMOTIONS

Table of Contents

When You're...

GRUMPY

By Naci Sigler

When I'm grumpy and unhappy...

When I'm a little tired too...

I don't feel like talking to you!

I just need some
alone time.

Later, I'll be
just fine.

The End

When You Need to...

CALM DOWN

By Naci Sigler

Have you ever sat down in a huff?

Aren't feeling too happy so you want to play too rough?

Or did you just get mad and blow up?

Something's definitely bothering you.
That's clear enough.

So, let's calm down
and talk this out.

Breathe deep and
relax so you
don't freak out.

Do you know what this is about?

Do you need to cry
to get it all out?

Or maybe just some space
to be mad or sad and pout?

Remember: Everything will always work itself out.

You'll feel better soon without a doubt.

The End

When You Need to Feel Better...

When Someone You Love Dies...

By Naci Sigler

I noticed that you're looking sad today.

Is it because you
loved had to
go forever away?

When someone you love is gone, it's normal to feel lost and alone.

It's always hard when someone we love dies...

All we want
to do is cry.

I wish there was some
magic words I could say…

to make it all better now.
But, eventually you'll be
okay.

Know that there's people
right here loving and
hurting for you...

So let me know if there's
anything we can do.

To help you see this sad
time through.

The End